CountryMusic ★ Stars
FAITH HILL

By Shelby Braidich

Gareth Stevens
Publishing

Please visit our Web site www.garethstevens.com. For a free color catalog of all our high-quality books, call toll free 1-800-542-2595 or fax 1-877-542-2596.

Library of Congress Cataloging-in-Publication Data

Braidich, Shelby, 1971-
Faith Hill / Shelby Braidich.
    p. cm. — (Country music stars)
Includes index.
ISBN 978-1-4339-3614-2 (pbk.)
ISBN 978-1-4339-3615-9 (6-pack)
ISBN 978-1-4339-3613-5 (library binding)
1. Hill, Faith, 1967—Juvenile literature. 2. Country musicians—United States—
Biography—Juvenile literature. I. Title.
ML3930.H53B73 2010
782.421642'092—dc22
[B]
                              2009040604

Published in 2010 by Gareth Stevens Publishing
111 East 14th Street, Suite 349
New York, NY 10003

Copyright © 2010 Gareth Stevens Publishing

Designer: Daniel Hosek
Editor: Greg Roza

Photo credits: Cover (background) Shutterstock.com; cover (Hill), title page © Kevin Mazur/WireImage/Getty Images; p. 5 © Paul Hawthorne/Getty Images; pp. 7, 27 © Larry Busacca/Getty Images; pp. 9, 15 © Kevin Winter/Getty Images; p. 11 © M. Caulfield/WireImage/Getty Images; p. 13 © Marianne Todd/Getty Images; p. 17 © Ron Galella/WireImage/Getty Images; p. 19 © David Drapkin/Getty Images; p. 21 © Evan Agonstini/Getty Images; p. 23 © Carlo Allegri/Getty Images; p. 25 © NBA Photos/Getty Images; p. 29 © Mike Nelson/AFP/Getty Images.

Printed in the United States of America

CPSIA compliance information: Batch #CW10GS: For further information contact Gareth Stevens, New York, New York at 1-800-542-2595.

CONTENTS

MISSISSIPPI GIRL

Faith Hill is a country music singer.

She was born on September 21, 1967.

Faith grew up in the small town of Star, Mississippi. She loved to sing when she was a child.

RISING STAR

Faith sang in her church choir when she was young.

9

Faith learned to play the guitar when she was a teen.

Faith started her own country music band when she was about 16.

Faith moved to Nashville, Tennessee, in 1987. She wanted to start a singing career.

15

FIRST ALBUMS

Faith put out her first album in 1993.

It was called *Take Me as I Am*.

Country music fans loved *Take Me as I Am*. Faith became famous!

19

Faith put out her second album in 1995. It was called *It Matters to Me*.

21

FAITH AND TIM

In 1996, Faith went on tour with a country singer named Tim McGraw. Faith and Tim have made several songs together.

23

Faith and Tim were married in 1996!

They have three daughters.

HIT SONGS

Faith has many hit singles. Her song "This Kiss" became famous all over the world.

AWARD WINNER

Today, Faith is still one of the most famous country music stars. She has won many awards.

TIMELINE

1967 Faith is born.

1984 Faith starts her own country music band.

1987 Faith moves to Nashville, Tennessee.

1993 Faith puts out *Take Me as I Am*.

1995 Faith puts out *It Matters to Me*.

1996 Faith gets married to Tim McGraw.

FOR MORE INFORMATION

Books:

Lindeen, Mary. *Cool Country Music: Create & Appreciate What Makes Music Great!* Edina, MN: ABDO Publishing Company, 2008.

Riggs, Kate. *Country Music.* Mankato, MN: Creative Education, 2008.

Web Sites:

CMT.com: Faith Hill
www.cmt.com/artists/az/hill_faith/artist.jhtml

Faith Hill
www.faithhill.com

GLOSSARY

award: a prize given to someone for doing something well

career: the job someone chooses to do for a living

choir: a group of people who sing together, especially in church

hit single: a song that is played a lot and liked by many people

tour: a trip to many places in order to entertain people

INDEX